St Eisenberg

and the

Sunshine Bus

Annick Yerem

First published 2022 by The Hedgehog Poetry Press

Published in the UK by
The Hedgehog Poetry Press
5, Coppack House
Churchill Avenue
Clevedon
BS21 6QW

www.hedgehogpress.co.uk

ISBN: 978-1-913499-90-7

Cover Illustration © Aurelia MacKenna Sales

Author Photograph © Barbara Dietl

Contents

When blurbs become their own poem- an introduction

This is:
A book of ingredients
A recipe for tenderness

A small strip of wonder
A burst of chaos and creation

It is
Support
Measured in flour, raisins, slivered almonds

A prayer
And *a handful of dirt*

This is
Time travel
Dripping goodbye

Shelves
Of *star-crushed birds*

Rainbow ends
In *chambers*
Filled with words

Achy
Sore
Unbroken

Robins, rainbows, starfish trails
BEWARE!

Nothing dies

Absence
more vivid and alive
than its prior occupants

Quiet now
Listen

Let heat transform you
Then let go

Craig Wedren, Musician, Composer, Artist

January 1st, 2020

I did not know
what lay ahead
when we tried to find our
way home the morning
of what would become
that year

How the world would shift
then break in all the wrong
places without you in it

I did not know

you would travel beside me
your tea tin my roadmap my safety
my tragic lucky charm
you would haunt the house
the heavens lifetimes ahead of me

in all your ghost and glimmer

a remembrance

for pepe

1.

what i know

my daughter has chestnut
eyes and seaweed hair

she is 5 or 10 or 50

i hold whole worlds inside
my stitched-up head
otters riddles
my collected lifetimes

today i woke up singing

so much more that
i could do right now
so much less

2.

welthaltig

sei bedeutend
und welthaltig

your everyday goodbye

no real translation
something someone
enfolds the world

when i was young i held
in the palm of my hand
the wonders the heartbreaks
the trees

if i breathed they could disappear

you don`t say it anymore
but i do i whisper it through
the ghost of your beard through
the scars on your scalp

3.

the making

everyone dies but
not everyone dies right?

take chopin you`ll see
my fingers trace the music
on the grand piano
darkening our living room

wish on blossoms during sakura season
look at pictures of me in kumamoto
drunk and happy writing
tanaka is crazy on a blackboard

think of us building shacks on
the beach a father-daughter dance
of shells and sand and driftwood

i need to remember you
i´m still listening still here

look at me look at everything

i gave you all the words
i collected all those worlds
in the making

Shelves

After Vicki Feaver

You are not here, nor in your bare room.
[*Shelves are forever*, inedible chocolates, forgotten pens,
two calendars, months behind]

Not in Berlin, wandering around museums
with F., eating cake, telling him what makes the
world go round [*sagenhaft* is a story is a memory is a sigh]

Latvia, Cambridge, Uzbekistan [where is a Silk Road when you need one],
Japan, Freiberg, Ludwigsburg, St. Charles, Ulm.
You are not [going to see your mum, your dad, your long-
dead sister, the girl bear]

Burning down all the houses you have ever lived in,
all the bridges that could lead to us.

You are not writing to me
nor cutting out silly pictures to me laugh
[shooting possums into space],
always in black felt pen, almost illegible
[signed D.P. So undercover]

You are [here], you are [not].

let april be april

tripped over memory lane
howling at the pink

moon my emerald
nettles your polkadot
starlings our brokenblue hearts

once upon a time i
hoped i was invincible

now there are shrikes and thorns
gathering around my worried
kingdom

Traces

The one on my nose
where I fell off a sleigh
then slid down an icy hill
and cut my face open

The one on my upper thigh
where I fell off my bed onto
a tambourine and
a bell burrowed
itself into my leg

The one on my chin
where the neighbour`s Dalmatian
whose name was Moritz
saw a German Shepherd on the other
side and dragged me across the road

The one on my upper lip
where my friend`s baby pulled on the
cast-iron pagoda in our
living room and smashed it
into my mouth

The ones on my belly
where they cut and prodded again
and again I have no words
for those

The one on my back
where they made me Titangirl
and one of my superpowers
was to tie my own shoelaces
after a month

The ones where you died
long before you died

and I was your witness

Hospital reports

1. The patient fell

2. The patient fell and split his head on a cupboard in his house

3. The patient fell and went to visit his wife with a bleeding head

4. The patient is a danger to others, also to himself

5. The patient tried to strangle his wife. He thought he was in a fight

6. The patient believes his daughter is out to get him

7. The patient fell. He fell again

8. The patient talked a lot about autonomy

9. The patient said he was a wreck

10 .The patient fell. He fell again

11. The patient loved his carers

12. His daughter knows they loved him back

13. The patient lost almost everything

But not them. Not her.

Japan Covid-19 officials cut off thousands of roses to deter gatherings *

Rest, sit down, have a sip of
sea tea, watch the birds hum through a crisp
morning.

This blooming world is out of kilter,
a frayed thing where flowers have to die
to shield us from their beauty

* https://www.theguardian.com/world/2020/apr/24/very-painful-japan-covid-19-officials-cut-off-thousands-of-roses-to-deter-gatherings

Seeing Things

Hallucinations are   *a side effect*
                         a sign of
decline

                       threatening
      people
thinking   *under*   *stress*
                           low
light
increase   *dark areas*
hallways
                    the form of
      light
or dogs.[1]

You are sitting on the bed of your 5th floor
hospital room, looking out into
the dark, preaching to a non-existent choir

      Ladies and Gentlemen, welcome to this lesson.
      A., you can only stay if you contribute.
      No slouching around, no chatting.

---

[1] https://www.parkinson.org ` More about Hallucinations `

16

I have written letters to your doctors
who do not care. I have brought towels from
home, because you were drying your hands
with one of your vests

> *Why are you doing this to me?*
> *We were just in Morocco and we were fine,*
> *apart from the fact that you always wanted to do your own thing,*
> *but that´s nothing new*

Morocco is far away. No-one here has ever
been to Morocco. I want you to feel Moroccan
heat, sand under your feet, drink mint tea thick
with sugar your spoon can stand in

> *You´re so ungrateful, always were.*
> *Where is my wife? Why is she hiding?*
> *How could she leave me here?*

Let me use your knife to sharpen my teeth,
call it truth. We are what we
see, wasn´t that the saying

> *We are what we see, wasn´t that the saying?*
> *Let me sharpen my truth, call it a knife,*
> *carry it between my teeth*

We live here too

for Alina

I have yet to write about the mice in the kitchen,
about how I painted red all the traps he had
laid out and wrote *BEWARE!* on them in
mouse code found in a tiny book under
the floorboards

Lately I haven´t been able to sleep.
I cry through the pain, I cry for
the world, I cry for the mice
and for everything that breaks me

I envy you, I say to the mice,
your grace and smallness, your
pinpointpearl eyes, your dashing
little feet. I envy your foreverprincess dances
when the cats have left the building, when
all the crumbs in the world are yours
to find, to keep. I envy your tips and toes
and crazy sprints, your woes, your willful ignorance
of traps. *Beware!* I say, of us, our human, trap-laying
form, of our anguish, our feebleness,
our anger, our hearts, our hurts

I go and lie down, just for a second,
and the mice huddle around me and sing me to sleep,
with lullabies of cheese and peanut dreams and dancing

St.Eisenberg & The Sunshine Bus

I am sure now that you were sending me signs

Heavens opened and closed, heat blazed
through me. The smell of freshly poured
tar on the motorway, turbines, sunflowers,
left right center

We stopped for a break near parched
woods, found raspberry gifts, barley
spikelets, wispy and gleaming like fairy hair

The damp, green quiet after a big rain,
fog hanging low in the mountains,
blurred brake lights

Midway, I lay down in a parking lot, crying
on my dog`s blanket, trying to make sense
of what we were doing

You were sending me signs:
robins, rainbows, star fish trails

That day, we drove towards your body,
to that uncluttered, bright space which enclosed
your darkness in those last, long years

That room where, when you left, someone
opened the vast window, so that your soul
could find its way out

Fifty

When I was little, we went to pick
brambles on our walks along
the vineyards, where lizards rustled
in stonewalls & tiny bats hid in hollows

I would stomp in, all business and curls,
then emerge covered in bloody scratches, bramble
juice and pride, triumphantly offering my harvest

Today`s walk is with my son, slowly
because of the August heat, reaching for
the brambles higher up, standing on my toes
like a ballerina, grabbing the juiciest ones,
the ones out of reach

You are gone.

Here´s the sun on my back, the nettles stinging
my legs, the branches ripping
my trousers, my heart.

Burial

We found him in the woods of the hospital grounds
across the road where we had gone to play

Bored by counting cars cause there weren`t enough
Empty parking lot after empty parking lot,
save for the one next to the building at the very end
where lots of people were coming and going

most of them wearing masks like we had seen on TV,
when our mum thought we weren`t watching

He was lying on his back, *eyes turned toward heaven,*
Mhairi said, but that was a lie cause you couldn`t even see
his eyes. Do red crayfish have eyes? I really don`t know

Someone had put him in an open jar in the middle of the woods,
had put some grass in that jar, a feather, a soft bed

He was lying there all still and shiny and we felt sad for him,
so we sang a song and cried a little
and did what we had seen the grownups do:

we dug a hole with our hands, lowered him into it and
said goodbye with a handful of dirt, grass

and a prayer

12.8.20

The world, the clocks, the telephones won`t stop.
Around the church, it smells of figs and holidays.
My bones hurt from all the unhugged hugs.
I step out of this cool church into godforsaken,
sizzling August heat, hold my head sideways
under a cold tap on my way to your
lavender peace, cry at your shadeless grave

Hair dripping goodbye
Your forever summer cold
Open hands empty

1.6.1983, Birthday Otters

Thank you for the wee otter book
you made for my birthday, *Pumpel.*
I like your gawky teenage writing
and that you did some proper research
(it`s a teacher thing).

Now you know why I adore otters.
Isn´t it great that their pelt is the thickest
of any mammal? The top layer which is waterproof,
then an underlayer to keep warm.

If I believed in rebirth,
I would like to be reborn as an otter.

My throat still hurts from the harsh words
spoken a few days ago.
Why do we fight all the time?
It was easier when you were little.

Otters are amazing, but so are you,
darling daughter, I hope you know that.

Beyond all the noise,
I just want to love you.

Home Otters

The whole family
roped in with your obsession:
posters, photos, t-shirts
books, visits to otter stations
old-school research.

And you were right, they are appealing:
they lie on their back, holding each other
chirping, grunting, chuckling
playing, fighting

A baby sea-otter´s cry sounds like a sea-gull.
Did you know that? Did you want to?
Maybe not, but that`s beside the point

You take all the wrong turns and make them
your place in the world which is full of
schmucks, you`d declare. Not otters though,
they´re good in everything they do.

Of all the lessons, these I´m grateful for:

how to cherish otters,
how to cherish words,
how to have a voice.

July 2020, Funeral Otters

Dear A.

Now is the time to say thank you
for all the otter stuff you gave
me over the years

As you know I´m always right so hear
me when I say I´ve learnt so
much from you maybe more than you
from me (although I don`t quite believe that)

The last few years were hard on both of us
but I heard your stories of otters
juggling with rocks while floating
sea otters using tools to break
open their food

I always knew they were just as clever as us
you never believed me

Thank you for bringing these presents
the otter postcard from all three of you
my favourite otter shirt tobacco pipe
I feel like a pharaoh showered with gifts
for a safe passage

I left a message for you
between the lavender in our garden
In case you don`t find it
here`s what it says

It´s too late for me to be saved
But I would like to be remembered

After Otters

My timeline graced with otters.
sliding around in the snow,
rolling around on ice cubes,
cracking them with their teeth.

The German post made a stamp,
shortly after you died, with an otter on it.
I put it on the envelopes of all
the thank-you cards. Otters vocalize,
they even cry. I did.

Our father-daughter mess,
a recipe for tenderness, disaster,
boiled-over grief and anger
and those heavens between us
I cannot fathom.

I´ve sold the house, but saved
your notes, my book,
newspaper clippings of
all things otter.

We echo things you said,
we say your special words out loud
to keep you alive, we keep you alive
through all the otters

You´d love that.
I loved you.

German Bake Off, home edition

The signature bake: how your mother/sister baked it, Swabian Cheesecake. Short crust pastry, no soggy bottoms, no frills, always real *Quark*. Mornings after parties, when breakfast was leftover *Fleischküchle*,[2] potato salad (no mayonnaise!), cake.

Never a technical: you turned our nose up at the hodge-podge of variations I offered over the years (but always tried and finished them, once on your plate). A crumbled-biscuit base seemed wrong, cream cheese a stretch. Who needs ill attempts at fruit-mirror-glaze?

The showstopper: 30 years of moving away from you and now I´m back here, wishing for raisins, wishing for rain, making promises I cannot keep, but still you hold them like the cake itself, admiring my work. Lemon-zest, a little custard powder, the maze-like imprint when you tip it onto a cooling-rack.

During our last phone call, you said *"Jetzt pass mal auf dich auf"*,[3] three times, like a spell. A mad dash of vanilla, copious amounts of tears. Now watch it turn golden through the oven door. Now let heat transform it. Now let it go.

---

[2] Swabian meatballs
[3] Take care of yourself now

Monrepos

We are standing on the steps that lead
Down to the murky lake.
I am small, red-coated, wild-curled.
I cannot yet pronounce Monrepos, but I love castles
and the stone lions I stroke into life each time we visit.

My mother´s hair is longer than I ever remembered,
my father is wearing his duffle coat,
I am slowly poisoning ducks with stale bread.

I want to remember him holding on to me.
If he lets go, are we still a family?

She is

the one that needs me,
I know because she tells
me so. I run and sniff,
cross meadows and
rivers, she makes
paths for me, always

She says I`m a good boy
and all the tasty things
just prove it

This year, she cried a lot
into my fur
(I´m not complaining),
but I want her to know
it`s no use crying over spilled
milk (I can help with that)
dead people, pain.

I want her to know
she`s a good girl,
I want her to smell the
love, the pee, the
flowers

Dance

I was scared of the drive home,
hundreds of kilometres towards
the second funeral in five weeks,
so you went to the best baker
in town, got me a sweet braided
loaf, support measured in flour,
raisins, slivered almonds

But when you unpacked it,
a dead bee was baked into the crust,
fully preserved as if poured in resin,
its blossom dreams halted in flight
forever.

At least it died happy, you said
and I imagined that bee, doing
one last waggle dance, wanting
to share the lemony sweetness
with all the other bees, dancing
as if its life depended on them
to find it before the heat came.

I left it on there and during the drive
opened the window, peeled it off
and let it fly, one last time, near
flowers, near trees, dancing,
twirling and the next moment

gone, just gone.

November walk

It´s the first cold day.
I breathe icicles over the canal
with my nine-lives dog
who is strutting along like a show pony,
all unbridled joy, his tail tick-tocking
like a metronome

To our left, an industrial complex,
hard-hatted figures roaming the
halls like playmobile people.

Next to a huge parking-garage, someone
has made a long, narrow garden.
Diligently stacked firewood, raised beds
with frosted tomatoes, a picnic table,
a bench (who would sit there?)

The way back will be guided by hot air balloons,
by freshly ploughed fields, herons, geese,
screeches from the nearby bird sanctuary.

I will be counting my sunny, cold,
beautiful blessings

But later that day, what I will think of
is this small strip of wonder, that burst of
chaos and creation, these
hopeful tomatoes.

i am a firm believer in fairy lights

the way they offer a twinkly hope
for better days, the way they cut
through the fog on winter nights,
illuminated landing strips
sparkling my walks round
the neighbourhood

an assembly of wayward, tiny stars

ages ago, you handed me a small
bundle and on the wrapping paper
you had written: `those dark corners
don`t stand a chance`

i switch them on at night
and every time i remember how
good it felt to know

that every once in a while
someone will see all your darkness
and help you light it up.

Beyond

1.

Danced on your grave when the sky fell, to remind you of the
living, who you were before the haunting started.
A breaking down of skins, shelves behind shelves where all
the truths were hidden.
Never knew you `till I knew you, did the puzzle,
made the pieces fit.

2.

The future is February fog, losing track of
all the hurts, no way to hunt them down.
The future is a sliver of time,
unlived, unheard of.
Quiet now, listen.

Magnolia

Last summer I watered your trunk
with concentration and care
but never touched your bark

I raked piles of leaves in autumn, bending
under moss-covered, low hanging
branches, preparing for a winter,
preparing for the first spring
my father will not see.

When the whole garden will be lit up
by billowing blossoms, fragrant to
the touch

After all the boxes were packed,
the curtains taken down,
the house stripped of its ghosts,
I went into the garden, put my ear to the ground
and waited to hear you say goodbye,
to hear you say you will remember them
and me.

Survival

after Adedayo Agarau

We fall like star-crushed birds,
like wildwoods, ice-sugared trees

We fall like polished shards of glass, like
crackling static, nauseated airwaves

Sing sundrenched hills
sing heather-lit havens
sing aching tender

kindness, sing

We fall too often like rain

Like shadows beneath it,
breathing us under

One-year prayer

after Anne McMaster

A year is a breath, she writes. *Only that.*

Saltwatered coasts
Swallows kiss bramble paths goodnight
Not-yet-smooth pebbles bejewel each step
Chamomile meadows drink in rainbow ends

Only a breath since I handed
last flecks of you to an indifferent sea

The heart of the matter

I never thought about your heart
(or mine), now it amazes me.
Atria, ventricles exchanging blood,
valves separating the two,
the endocardium protecting
both valves and chambers

I imagine your chambers
filled with books, with words,
with the heat of arguments,
the ghosts of them wandering
through now-foreign corridors

When everything failed, this
held you together, it´s as
simple as that. Your aortic valve
just kept your blood flowing in
the right direction.

Until it didn`t.

On the echocardiogram, my heart
looks like a Francis Bacon painting,
like one of Marc Quinn´s self portraits
made out of his own blood.
My heart ache, my heart sore.
It does not look broken.

Look, the cardiologist says,
how fragile, how tender your heart is.
Just like you.

I step into summer with my bleeding heart,
the yearning, breathing loss of yours
and offer it to sparrowed skies.

Acknowledgements:

Thank you to Mark from Hedgehog Press for choosing to publish this journey & for welcoming me into the hoglet family.
Thank you to the editors of the following journals, presses, literary magazines, podcasts & blogs. Some of the words in this book were previously published by
DREICH, detritus, Anti-Heroin Chic, Poet Rhy Garden project, iamb, Poetry in Public, Feral, Sledgehammer Lit, Bale of Joy, Eat The Storms podcast, Sarah Connor´s Advent Calendar, Wombwell Rainbow

Thank you to
Nancy Wigglesworth for being an amazing coach. This book would not exist without you.
Tara Skurtu for delightful tutoring & for the International Poetry Circle
Wendy Pratt & Jonathan Davidson for inspiring workshops & courses

Aurelia MacKenna Sales for my dream cover
Barbara Dietl for the amazing photos over the years

To the best poet-friends anyone could hope for. I am in awe of your talent & your kindness:

Ankh Spice for sending words, love, flowers & goat songs from the sea
My beautiful Flaming Flowers Giovanna MacKenna, Sandra Birnie, Britt Doughty-Godchaux, Susan Jack, for sharing words, laughter, tears & Tunnocks with me for the past two years & for being brilliant, gorgeous & gracious Lindsey Heatherly for being wonderful, Damien Donnelly for the unwavering support & the laughter, Anne Mc Master for seeing beauty wherever she goes & for the support, Rhona Greene for her amazing heart, Sarah Connor for the letters & poems, Kate Dowling for the letters & colours, JP Seabright for the safe space, Alina Stefanescu for the mice, Claire Marsden for being my moonbound endosister. Sarah-Jane Crowson for her art & her tech wizardry, Debbie Ross for the kindness, Lynn Valentine for words & dogs, Gaynor Kayne for the encouragement.

MI, Rachel, Mo, Peach, Sage, David, Alessa Paul, James, Julie, Sam, Sue, Anindita, Devon, Wendy J. Oormila, Taylor & many more. I appreciate you so much.
Vicki Feaver, for "You Are Not"
Adedayo Agarau, for "The Gods Ask Us To Make An Oasis"
Anne Mc Master for that amazing line

Tanya Shadrick for being fabulous & kind
Stefanie Rixecker for the encouragement when I got started
Valerie Coffin Price for the lovely chats & your art
Cate Spice for the seawitching
Craig Wedren for being a part of the soundtrack of my life

Sabine for decades of friendship & believing in me
Lilo for helping me help myself when I couldn´t
Susanne for being who she is

My parents, Kate and Hansjörg, for all the words that shaped me

Andreas, my partner in crime, for seeing me all this time. We are still here.

And to Fynn, my North Star. This is for you.

"The poetry of grief is often fragile, holed by loss. Yerem's work is the tree in the flash flood that stays upright. Her poems are steeped in the baffle of wonder and persistence – and nourished by the same source that batters, to burst forth spring leaves, berries, birds, hopeful tomatoes, bedecked with fairy lights, shading children and dogs, moments of memory and surely of future-despite, each one brighter for the devastation. This collection is a tender and raw tribute to her father, and the gap of him is painted in every colour of ache by Yerem's skill for new ways to say missing:

...we drove towards your body,
to that uncluttered, bright space which enclosed
your darkness in those last, long years...

... preparing for the first spring
my father will not see.

Yet it is far more - a making-sense of how to stay standing, deeply and unfairly alive, full of sway, waving every flag that spells out 'how to love this world' the missing one so clearly handed her. Yerem's unique voice has profoundly strong roots – this is a poet writing from the very middle of the deluge of feeling, gathering to herself all that persists between reminders that there is an end for all of us, but nothing takes what we give:
everyone dies but
not everyone dies right?
Yerem's skill is urgent and fresh, her artful, often impish cadence invites you to dance with her despite every hurt. If you've realised grief is what it costs us to love, if you know it's always worth the price, this beautiful first collection from a poet-to-watch, one who writes on the darkest road with pure sunshine, is for you:

every once in a while
someone will see all your darkness
and help you light it up."

Ankh Spice poet, *The Water Engine*, co-editor Ice Floe Press

"Annick Yerem writes with such beauty, strength and
surprising turns of language about familial love and loss.
These are poems to read aloud, learn by heart and share
with those we hold dear."

Tanya Shadrick, artist& writer, *The Cure For Sleep*

"Here, Annick Yerem shares her efforts to make sense of
the world after her father's death. In this liturgy of poems,
Yerem picks at the scars left by the work of grieving for the
not-yet-dead, examines the surprising shapes that hold the
fragility of our most precious relationships, and pins down
the fragments we clutch to keep our dead with us. In this
collection, love is translated through the fascination of an
animal - the overwhelm of the emotion kept at a safe remove
by its broken journey but left no less powerful for it. These
poems look unflinchingly at how our place in the world
shifts following the death of those who made us, the
touchstone of nature giving foundation to that loss.
This is a beautiful, affecting work which will be felt by all
who have ever felt grief."

Giovanna MacKenna, Poet, How the Heart can Falter

About Annick Yerem

Annick Yerem was born in Japan to German/ Scottish parents and is always slightly homesick for Scotland. She is a poet, a teacher, a carer and Mum to a very tall human who understands maths and physics a lot better than she does. Annick is an avid-dog lover (and emerging dog whisperer) and a big fan of Podencos,, Highland cattle and manatees as well as a renowned cake spy. Her goal is to uplift and support other writers and artists as much as she possibly can and to have fun while she´s at it. She is a member of the Flaming Flower Society.

You can find out more about Annick´s work here:

https://annickyerem.wordpress.com

Lightning Source UK Ltd.
Milton Keynes UK
UKHW010656290822
408013UK00002B/372